Tilda's SPRING IDEAS

Tone Finnanger

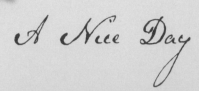

A Nice Day

Spring is in the air; time for a garden party with good friends and blissful uninterrupted hours in the sewing workroom. It is going to be a great day. There is nothing better than having time to spend on what you like best, your friends and your hobby.

Here you will find two chapters filled with beautiful projects inspired by springtime. In the first chapter, Garden Party, you will find new angels sporting trouser suits, denim jackets and crochet summer hats, plus gorgeous décor ideas and festive bags. You will also meet Bug, a funny guy who takes care of the party's delicacies; too busy to worry about carbs and calories. The second chapter, Sewing Workshop, introduces us to a sewing angel inspired by Marilyn Monroe, with a cheeky bright red sewing machine. There are also lovely little storage boxes, cute sewing kits and my personal favourites; the pinwheels – easy is often better.

Best Regards,

Tone Finnanger

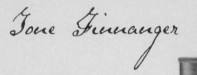

Tilda's
SPRING
IDEAS

Contents

A DAVID & CHARLES BOOK
© CAPPELEN DAMM AS 2012
www.cappelendamm.no

Originally published as *Tildas Varideer*
First published in the UK in 2012 by F&W Media International, LTD

David & Charles is an imprint of F&W Media International, LTD
Brunel House, Forde Close, Newton Abbot, TQ12 4PU, UK

F&W Media International, LTD is a subsidiary of F+W Media, Inc.
4700 East Galbraith Road, Cincinnati, OH 45236

Tone Finnanger has asserted her right to be identified as author of this work in accordance with the Copyright, Designs and Patents Act, 1988.

A catalogue record for this book is available from the British Library.

ISBN-13: 978-1-4463-0244-6 paperback
ISBN-10: 1-4463-0244-X paperback

Printed in China by RR Donnelley
for F&W Media International, LTD
Brunel House, Forde Close, Newton Abbot,
TQ12 4PU, UK

10 9 8 7 6 5 4 3 2 1

Illustrations: Tone Finnanger
Photography: Sølvi Dos Santos
Styling: Ingrid Skaansar
Book design: Tone Finnanger

F+W Media Inc. publishes high quality books on a wide range of subjects.
For more great book ideas visit: **www.rucraft.co.uk**

Stuffed Figures

SEWING

Avoid cutting out the parts for a stuffed figure freehand unless absolutely necessary. Fold the fabric double right sides facing, iron and transfer the pattern on to it, see figure A. Sew carefully and evenly along the marked lines, using a stitch length of approximately 1.5mm (⅝in).

CUTTING

Cut out the item with a narrow seam allowance of 3–5mm (⅛– ³⁄₁₆in) along the seams and 8–12mm (⁵⁄₁₆–½in) by the openings. Then cut a notch in the seam allowance where it curves sharply inwards.

REVERSING

Reverse the arms and legs by pushing the blunt end of a wooden stick against the tip of the arm/leg, see figure B. Start closest to the foot/hand and pull the leg/arm down along the wooden stick, see figure C. Continue to pull the leg down the stick until the tip of the foot/hand emerges from the opening. Pull the foot while drawing back the bottom so the leg/arm will be turned inside out, see figure D. Always iron reversed pieces. You can also use the blunt end of a wooden stick to help with stuffing. A good tip is to keep a selection of wooden sticks in different sizes for this purpose.

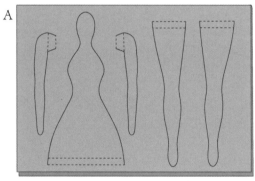

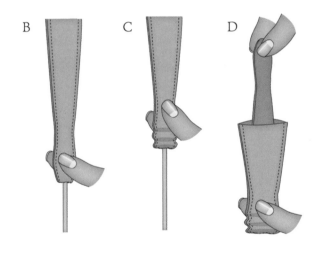

Appliqués

You will find little appliqué signs accompanying some of the models in this book, such as Bug (see pages 10–11) and the Sewing Kit (see pages 28–29). The signs are printed on fabric and can be bought from good Tilda suppliers. They are cut with a 7–10mm (¼– ⅜in) seam allowance. Cut little notches in the seam allowance where it curves sharply before you fold and tack (baste) so the edge around the sign will be as even as possible. The tacking (basting) stitches should be removed when the sign is attached to the model, so it is a good idea to use a bright red thread that is easy to see when you remove it.

Place the sign on the model and stitch around the edges using a thread colour that matches the sign so the stitches are hidden. Remove the tacking (basting) stitches from the seam allowance and iron the sign. Alternatively, the signs can be easily attached using double-sided fusible web, with or without using blanket stitches around the edges.

Face

Push two pins into the head to determine where the eyes should be placed. Remove the pins and fix the eyes into the pinholes using the eye tool from a face kit or a pinhead dipped in paint. Lipstick can be applied using a dry brush to create rosy cheeks when the eyes have dried.

Hair

Insert pins from the forehead down along the middle of the backside of the head. Then insert one pin on either side of the head. Twist hair back and forth between the pins on each side, and divide the hair between the pins in the middle, see figure E. When the head is covered, tack (baste) to attach the hair and remove the pins.

To make a lock of hair, attach the tip of a long "strand of hair" to the head with a long thread. Place the blunt end of a wooden stick against the head where the thread and hair are attached. Make sure the thread is lying against the wooden stick and twist four or five times around the stick and thread, see figure F. Carefully detach the hair from the stick and attach with a couple of stitches, making use of the thread that is already through the locks.

Do not cut thread or hair, but continue to the next lock, see figure G. Continue until you have about eight or nine locks.

If you would like to include a hair bobbin, avoid making locks where this should be attached.

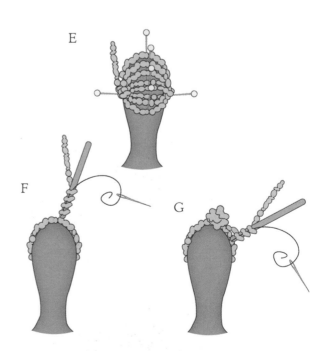

E

F

G

Garden Party

Get ready for the garden party! Gorgeous angels in casual bohemian style with cute butterfly hats and cool denim jackets adorn the picnic tables whilst "Bug" is walking around checking on the food. With cute cupcake garlands, floral party bags and beautiful dog roses decorating the tables, the décor is pleasing to the eye.

Bug

YOU WILL NEED
Fabric for the body
Fabric for the wings
Skin coloured fabric for
the face
Double-sided fusible web
Insert wadding
Wadding (batting)
Thin steel wire
Buttons

HOW TO MAKE

BODY

Fold the fabric for the body double right sides facing and trace the figure from the pattern. Sew all the way around and strengthen by sewing a double seam by the neck, under the arms and between the legs.

Cut the figure and cut notches in the seam allowance where the seam turns inwards. Make the reversing opening through one of the fabric layers as marked in the pattern, see figure A. Reverse the figure, using a flower stick or similar to reverse the arms and legs more easily, then iron the figure.

Stuff the figure firmly using wadding (batting) to achieve a nice shape. Close the opening using tacking (basting) stitches.

Iron double-sided fusible web against a piece of the skin fabric and pull off the paper. Trace and cut the face from the pattern and iron it to the head.

Sew blanket stitches around the face if you wish.

COLLAR

Cut a strip of fabric to measure 30 × 4cm (12 × 1½in), adding a seam allowance. Iron in the seam allowances and fold the strip in half to measure 30 × 2cm (12 × ¾in).

Sew with large stitches along the open edge and pucker the stitching to create a clown collar effect.

Attach the collar around the neck using tacking (basting) stitches.

WINGS AND ANTENNAE

Fold the fabric for the wings double right sides facing and place insert wadding (batting) underneath. Trace and sew around the wings. Cut and make a reverse opening through one of the layers as marked in the pattern, reverse and iron. Glue or tack (baste) on the wings so the reverse opening on the wings is turning in towards the reverse opening at the back.

Cut a small piece of thin steel wire to 30cm (12in). Push a doll needle or similar through the top of the head to create an opening, see figure B, then carefully insert the steel wire. Thread a button on to both ends of the steel wire. Decide a suitable length for the antennae before you twist the wire around itself underneath the button and cut the ends.

Make a face as described on page 7.

A

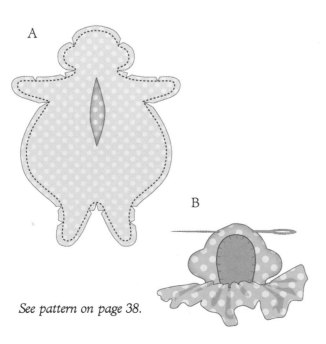

B

See pattern on page 38.

Springtime Bags

HOW TO MAKE
BAG
Note that the pattern is divided in two pieces to fit the pattern page. Put the pieces together by lining up points A and B. Double the pattern to make both sides of the bag and mark with a folding edge.

Cut a piece of iron-on fusible interfacing equal to the whole pattern, lid included. Add a seam allowance around the bag, but not around the lid. Also cut a piece that equals the whole bag without the lid, adding a seam allowance around the whole bag except along the top edge.

Iron the fusible interfacing piece against the wrong side of the fabric you wish to use. Cut right next to the seam allowance at the fusible interfacing side around the bag, adding some extra seam allowance around the lid. Cut notches in the seam allowance around the lid.

Cut strips of double-sided fusible web, pull the adhesive from the paper and place the strips between the seam allowance when ironing, see figure A.

Repeat this method on the part without the lid, and iron in some extra seam allowance using iron-on double-sided fusible web along the top edge.

Place the two parts right sides facing and stitch together on each side and at the bottom, see figure B. Fold opposite so the seams meet and stitch up the openings on each side to create a base, see figure C.

LINING
Sew the lining fabric in the same way as for the bag, but iron and tack (baste) the seam allowance around the lid and along the edge without double-sided fusible web.

Place the lining inside the bag so the wrong side of the lining is against the fusible interfacing. Sew around the lid and along the edge, see figure D. Iron the bag and lid into position.

YOU WILL NEED
Heavy-weight fusible interfacing
Fabric for the bag
Fabric for lining
Fusible interfacing
Fabric for a bow or a fringe (optional)
Press-stud button or a button-hole
   loop (optional)

BOW
Note that the pattern for the bow is marked with a folding edge and should be doubled. Fold the fabric for the bow right sides facing and trace the bow. Sew around, leaving a reverse opening in the seam, then cut, reverse and iron. Fold the bow, see figure E.

Cut a strip of fabric to 1.5cm (⅝in) plus seam allowance, fold in the seam allowance and tighten the fabric strip around the bow. Attach to the bag.

FRINGE
Tear a fabric strip to 3cm (1⅛in) × the fabric width, seam allowance included. Using a sewing machine, sew a 6mm (¼in) seam along one of the edges without attaching the thread. Pucker by pulling the thread until the strip ruffles to equal the perimeter of the lid.

Sew the strip to the underside of the lid so about 2cm (¾in) will show outside the edge. Remove loose threads. Use a press-stud button or a loop as a closing mechanism of the bag. Attach the press stud button as described in the manufacturer's instructions.

See pattern on page 39.

A

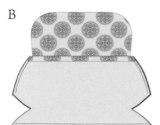

B

C

D

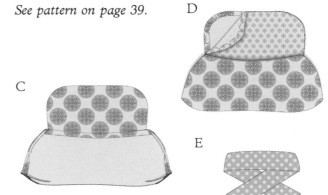

E

Garden Party Angels

HOW TO MAKE
BODY

Note that the patterns for the body and legs are divided to fit the pattern page. Put the pieces together by lining up points A and B. Fold the skin fabric right sides facing and trace a body, two arms and two legs. Sew around all the parts.

Cut out all of the parts and cut notches in the seam allowance where the seams are turning inwards. Reverse and iron the parts, then iron in the seam allowance on the body and arms.

Stuff the bottom part of the leg with wadding (batting) up to the thin, dotted line in the pattern. Sew a seam across the "knee" before you stuff the rest of the leg, see figure A.

Stuff the body and arms. Place the legs inside the body and baste, see figure B. The arms should be attached a little behind the chest so they are positioned leaning slightly back from the shoulders and closer to the body, see figure C.

TROUSER (PANT) SUIT

Cut a piece of fabric to measure 20 × 10cm (8 × 4in) for the top, adding a seam allowance. Fold the fabric double right sides facing to become 20 × 5cm (8 ×2in) broad, and sew along the open long side.

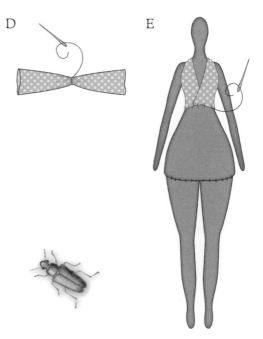

YOU WILL NEED
Fabric for the body
Fabric for the trouser suit
Fabric for the wings
Thin denim fabric
Tilda hair or similar
Wadding (batting)
White pearls 3–4mm
   (1/8in–5/32in)
Embroidery yarn or thin
   crochet yarn

Reverse and iron the top. Sew a seam across the middle and pucker, see figure D.

Attach the top so the puckered area is at the neck, and the ends overlap in front. Attach with a few stitches, see figure E.

See patterns on pages 40–43.

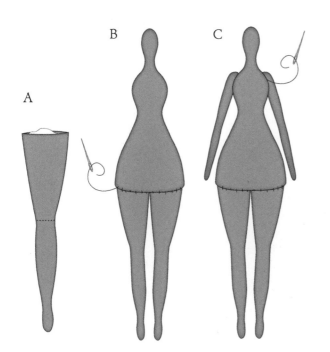

Note that the trouser pattern is divided to fit the pattern page. Place the parts together by lining up points A and B. The pattern is marked with a folding edge and should be doubled.

Cut two trouser parts, place them right sides facing and stitch up, see figure F. Fold the trousers opposite so the seams are lying over and under each other and stitch up the legs, see figure G.

Iron in the seam allowance by the openings for the legs then dress the trousers onto the angel. The trousers should be attached fairly high up on the waist. Fold two tucks in the front and two at the back and attach with tacking (basting) stitches. Tack (baste) around the edge of each opening and pucker the legs together around the angel's leg, see figure H.

DENIM JACKET

It is important to use a thin denim fabric for this jacket as it is very detailed. Here we have used Tilda denim fabric with white sewing thread for an authentic finishing touch.

Cut out a piece of fabric large enough for four pockets, fold twice and trace one of the two pockets from the pattern. Sew around, cut out, reverse and iron the pockets.

Cut out two front parts and one back part. Place the pockets on each front part and stitch in place, see figure I. Fold the pockets down and sew a seam to hold them in place, see figure J.

Fold the fabric for the collar twice, trace the collar from the pattern and sew around, see figure K. Cut, reverse and iron the collar. Sew a seam 3mm (⅛in) inside the edge with white sewing thread, see figure L.

Cut out two sleeves from the pattern. Sew the front pieces to the back piece by the shoulders and sew a sleeve on to each side, see figure M.

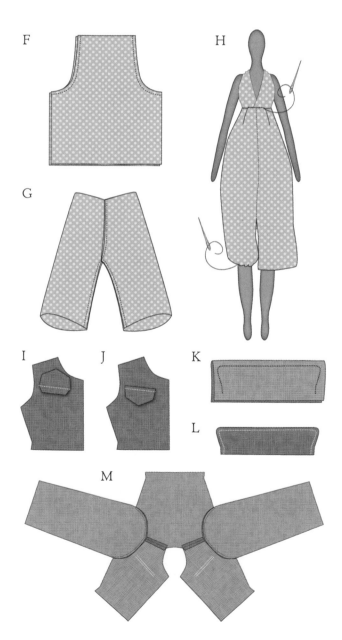

Fold up the seam allowance at the bottom of each sleeve and sew around. Fold the jacket right sides facing and stitch up underneath the sleeves on each side of the jacket, see figure N.

Cut a notch in the seam allowance close to the seam underneath the sleeves and in the curved seam allowance. This will avoid a stretch between the sleeves and shoulders when reversing. Iron the jacket.

Place the collar against the right side of the jacket, positioning the middle of the collar against the middle of the backside. Sew the collar to the jacket, see figure O. Fold and iron the collar upwards, so the seam is facing the inside of the jacket, before you fold the upper part of the collar down.

Iron in the seam allowance on each side by the openings at the front of the jacket and sew. Fold and iron in the seam allowance along the edge at the bottom of the jacket and sew, see figure P.

Sew little pearls as buttons on the pockets along the opening, see picture opposite. To make the decorative dog rose, see page 21.

Dress the jacket on to the figure. For the jacket to fit nicely, you can tack (baste) it to the figure where necessary.

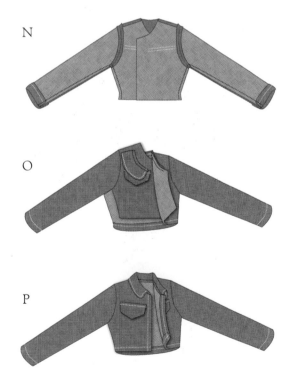

N

O

P

WINGS
Fold the fabric twice and trace the wings from the pattern. Sew around the wings, see figure Q. Reverse and iron the wings and sew the seams as marked in the pattern, see figure R. Stuff the wings by using a wooden stick and stitch up the opening, then tack (baste) the wings to the figure.

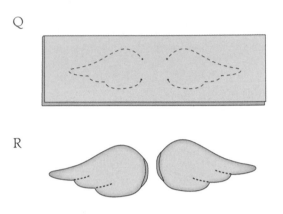

Q

R

CROCHET SUMMER HAT
If you do not wish to crochet a hat, make hair as described on page 7.

Embroidery yarn and a crochet hook number 2 are used to make these small, quick-to-make hats. Try to ensure that the threads do not separate. You can alternatively use thin crochet yarn, but you must measure the head first to size the hat correctly.

Make 24 ch (chain stitches) and make a circle.
1st round: Start the round with 1 ch and make 23 sc (single crochets). Finish with 1 sl st (slip stitch) in the 1st ch.
2nd round: Start the round with 2 ch – 1 dc (double crochet). Then crochet 23 dc. Finish with 1 sl st in 2nd ch.
3rd round: Start the round with 2 ch – 1 dc (double crochets). Crochet 23 dc. Finish with 1 sl st in 2nd ch.
4th round: Start the round with 2 ch – 1 dc. Crochet 1 dc, skip 1 dc, crochet 2 dc, skip 1 dc, and continue throughout the round.
Finish by pulling the yarn through the top crochet stitches and attach.

Place a few "strands of hair" inside the hat before you place it on the head to prevent the scalp from showing through the stitches. Make two large balls of hair and attach to each side of the head with pins before you tack (baste) in place.

Make face as described on page 7.

Dog Roses

YOU WILL NEED
Fabric for the rose petals
Pearls

HOW TO MAKE

Use 3 and 4mm (⅛ and ⁵⁄₃₂in) pearls for the small dog roses and 3 and 5mm (⅛ and ³⁄₁₆in) pearls for the larger ones.

Trace and cut petals from the pattern without adding a seam allowance. You will need five petals to make one flower.

Pull out a few loose threads around the edge of the flower petals to create a frayed fringe edge. Iron every petal folded in half wrong sides facing. Sew in the fold through a petal with large stitches and continue with the next petal, see figure A.

When you have finished, use the same thread to sew through all the petals, puckering them together carefully. Sew several rounds, pulling the thread gradually more tightly until the opening in the middle of the flower is as small as possible, see figure B. Stitch on the pearls alternating between attaching the large and small pearls to the folds around the edge.

The flowers can be used to decorate many projects, from brightening up dolls' clothing (see picture opposite) to embellishing a box or lampshade (see page 31).

See pattern on page 45.

A   B

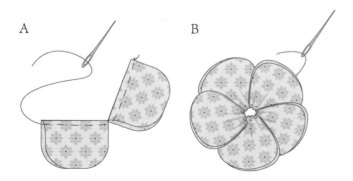

Gift Bags

YOU WILL NEED
Stiff scrapbook paper
Paper adhesive (an adhesive
   roller is recommended)
String for the handle
Utility knife
Ruler

HOW TO MAKE

Trace the pattern for the bag twice beside each other and finish with the flap to create a net for the box, see figure A.

Cut out the bag without including a seam allowance. Use a utility knife and ruler to mark all the folds indicated with a dotted line in the pattern.

Fold the top edge down, the flaps for the bottom up, and the mid folds on each side short side together with the adhesive flap inwards, see figure B. Apply paper adhesive to the adhesive flap and glue the bag together, then glue the flaps at the bottom together.

Make holes in the bag for the handles using a belt punch or similar and tie the strings to the bag.

See pattern on page 44.

A

B

Cupcake Garland

I'm always thinking about easy seasonal decoration ideas and was very happy when I came up with this pretty cupcake garland. With a great selection of cupcake liners available in a wide range of colours, they are a simple but effective material for this quick-to-make garland. Use a variety of liners and patterns or stick to just one type for a simpler design.

HOW TO MAKE
Flatten the cupcake liners and fold them twice wrong sides facing. Fold out again and apply a line of adhesive next to the fold on one side. Place the string in the central fold then fold the liner in half to stick in place. Repeat with your desired number of cupcake liners to create your garland.

YOU WILL NEED
String
Cupcake liners
Adhesive (an adhesive
   roller is recommended)

Sewing Workroom

If you have a great passion for needlework, nothing can compare with blissful undisturbed hours in the sewing workroom, by the dining table or wherever you have made room for your hobby. Here you will find ideas for sewing fanatics, including pin cushions, cute sewing kits and last but not least, a cheeky little sewing angel with a bright red sewing machine.

Pinwheels

HOW TO MAKE

Cut out a strip of fabric measuring 35 × 12.5cm (13¾ × 4⅞in), adding a seam allowance. Cut a strip of iron-on heavy-weight fusible interfacing measuring 35 × 2.5cm (13¾ × 1in), only adding a seam allowance to each short side so it remains 2.5cm (1in) wide.

Place the interfacing strip in the middle of the wrong side of the fabric strip with the adhesive side down. Iron and sew a seam along each long side of the interfacing strip, about 2mm (³⁄₃₂in) from the edge.

Iron in the seam allowance along each long side of the fabric strip and fold the strip double right sides facing. Stitch up the open side, see figure A and reverse so the right side is facing out.

Use embroidery yarn to sew around one of the edges and pucker to create the base of the pinwheel. Cut out a cardboard circle equal to the large circle in the pattern and push the cardboard down towards the bottom inside the pinwheel, see figure B.

Sew around the other edge. Stuff the pinwheel firmly with wadding (batting) before you pucker it together and attach the thread, see figure C. Steam with the iron to press the pinwheel into a flatter shape.

Fold a piece of fabric that is big enough for the smaller circle in the pattern twice right sides facing. Trace and sew around the circle. Cut out the circle and make a reversing opening through one of the layers. Reverse and iron.

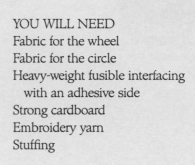

YOU WILL NEED
Fabric for the wheel
Fabric for the circle
Heavy-weight fusible interfacing
with an adhesive side
Strong cardboard
Embroidery yarn
Stuffing

Place the circle in the middle of the pinwheel on the opposite side to the cardboard base. Tack (baste) the circle using the same colour embroidery yarn to create invisible stitches.

Fold a ribbon in half and tack (baste) it to the underside of the pinwheel to act as a hanger.

See pattern on page 42.

See pattern on page 42.

A

B

C

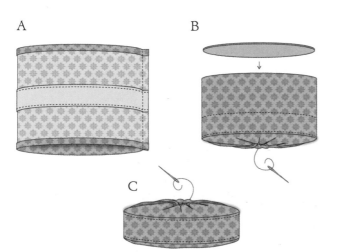

Sewing Kit

HOW TO MAKE

Trace and cut out a piece of iron-on heavy-weight fusible interfacing measuring 42 × 14cm (16½ × 5½in) without a seam allowance. Use a ruler to ensure that the corners are straight. Use a small bobbin or coin to draw a smooth curve in each corner and cut out. Make another piece the same way, but this should be 3mm (⅛in) shorter in length and height, i.e. 41.7 × 13.7cm (16⅜ × 5⅜in).

The largest piece will be the outside of the sewing kit. Place it with the adhesive side down towards the wrong side of your desired fabric and iron so the to attach the interfacing to the fabric.

Cut around the fabric, leaving a minimum of 1cm (⅜in) seam allowance of fabric outside the interfacing. Cut notches in the corners of the seam allowance.

Iron in the seam allowance. Strips of iron-on double-sided fusible web could possibly be used to attach the seam allowance. Sew with a large seam with a sewing machine to keep the seam allowance temporarily in place. Sew as tightly as possible around the edge if you are not using fusible web strips, ensuring that the seam is able to be removed.

Follow the same procedure with the smaller cut out part and the lining.

YOU WILL NEED
Heavy-weight fusible interfacing with an adhesive side
Fabric for the outside
Fabric for the lining
Strips of iron-on double-sided fusible web
Ribbon
Hook and loop fasteners

Place the lining precisely inside the other piece and fold together as you would for a finished sewing kit. Firstly, fold the right sides together, then fold the left side above. Adjust the folds in the right places, and iron to mark the folds.

Mark where the hook and loop fasteners should be placed in order for them to attach to each other, then fold the pieces out again.

Fold the fabric rights facing and trace a square measuring 16 × 10.5cm (6¼ × 4⅛in). Sew around. Cut out and make a small reverse opening through one of the layers in the middle of the square, then reverse and iron.

Fold and iron the square twice so you will have two pieces for needles, one about 9.5cm (3¾in) and the other about 6.5cm (2½in), with the reverse opening on the underside. Place the folded square in the middle of the piece furthest to the right on the lining and attach on top with a seam, see figure A.

A

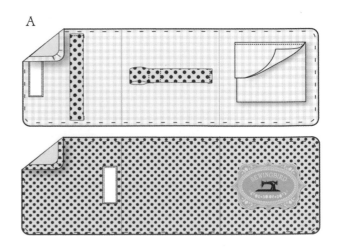

Use a wide ribbon to make loops tailored to fit your sewing equipment, see picture and figure A on pages 28–29. The end of the ribbon in the middle piece of the lining is folded in a way that creates a loose loop to hold scissors. Use your scissors to measure how large the loop should be before you start sewing.

Fold the tip of the ribbon in the opposite end and attach with a seam. You can sew as many seams as you wish to create the loops or space for your equipment. Attach the hook and loop fasteners.

Stitch on a fabric sign to the front side if you wish, see figure A on page 28 and Appliqués on page 6.

Finally, place the pieces wrong sides facing and stitch up with a seam about 3mm (⅛in) from the edge, see figure B.

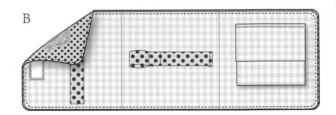

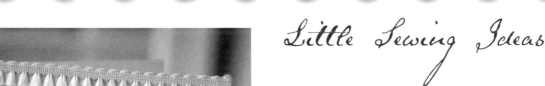

Little Sewing Ideas

PAPER SEWING EQUIPMENT

On page 45 you can find a selection of printable sewing motifs. These can be printed onto good quality sewing paper and glued onto patterned cardboard from Tilda paper pads or similar to create substantial models with a pretty backdrop.

Cut out the models. Fold a piece of fabric and attach it to the needle card using a stapler or similar to create a pretty needle case. The cards make lovely gift tags or can be used for storage for your nicest buttons. Simply sew the buttons to the card.

LAMP SHADE NOTICE BOARD

To create a three-dimensional alternative to the traditional notice board, dress an old lamp shade with 2cm (¾in) wide fabric strips. Attach the ends using a glue gun.

Among the Tilda products you can find paper and décor with a sewing theme, enabling you to make customised cards and decorate gifts for your friends.

See page 44 for gift tag pattern

Sewing Angel

HOW TO MAKE

DRESS

Follow the instructions for the Garden Party Angels on page 14 up to figure E, where the top of the trouser (pant) suit is attached.

Cut a piece of fabric measuring 66 × 30cm (25¾ × 12in) for the skirt, adding a seam allowance. Fold the skirt double right sides facing, making it 30cm (12in) in height and 33cm (13in) in width and stitch up the open side. Reverse the skirt, iron and sew the seam allowance at the bottom up.

Sew along the top edge of the skirt and pucker at the waist. Attach with a few stitches, see figure A.

BELT

Cut a piece of fabric measuring 6 ×30cm (2⅜ × 12in) without a seam allowance. Fold and iron 1cm (⅜in) inwards on each short side and 1cm (⅜in) along each long side, see figure B.

Fold and iron the strip twice to become 1.5cm (⅝in) wide and stitch up the open side, see figure C. Tie the belt tight around the waist. Attach the knot and upper part of the ends with a few stitches to secure and let the two ends hang down, see figure D.

YOU WILL NEED
Fabric for the skin
Fabric for the dress
Fabric for the wings
Fabric for piece of fabric
Mini bobbins
Tilda hair
Wadding (batting)
Thin wooden stick
Adhesive pads
Print of a sewing machine
Glue gun (optional)

Sew and attach the wings as described on page 18. Make the hair and face as described on page 7.

See patterns on pages 40–42.

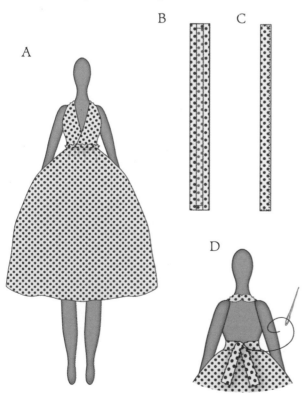

33

SEWING MACHINE

Print or photocopy the sewing machines from page 43 onto photo cardboard and cut out. Cut a piece of a thin wooden stick to approximately 10cm (4in).

Place the stick to the position that the bobbin is attached to on the sewing machine and attach adhesive pads around it, see figure E. Remove the paper from the adhesive pads and glue the other part of the sewing machine on to these. Thread the bobbin onto the stick, see figure F, using glue to secure if desired.

Cut a piece of fabric measuring 10 × 15cm (4 × 5¾in), adding a seam allowance. Fold the piece right sides facing to measure approximately 10 × 7.5cm (4 × 3in) and stitch up the long side and one of the short sides. Reverse and iron the piece. Fold a few tucks in the piece of fabric and bend it around the sewing machine so it will tack (baste) to itself in the back, see figure G.

The sewing machine can be attached to the angel's hands by carefully pushing the needle and thread between the adhesive pads between the two layers of the sewing machine when you tack (baste). Then attach the upper part of the sewing machine to the dress using tacking (basting) stitches around the bobbin attachment, see figure H. Alternatively, the easiest way is to use a glue gun.

E

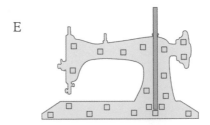

F

G

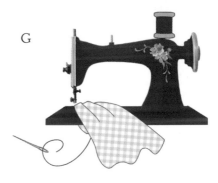

H

Fabric Boxes

HOW TO MAKE

Trace the pattern four times next to each other on iron-on heavy-weight fusible interfacing. Cut so you will have seam allowance on all sides except the top edge, see figure A.

Cut two pieces of fabric large enough for the whole shape, but add 1.5cm (⅝in) to the fabric strip for the lining and subtract the same on the fabric strip for the outside of the box. This will make a lining border on the outside of the box, see the picture opposite.

Stitch up the two fabric strips and iron a seam allowance in the splice away from each other.

Place the case interfacing piece with the adhesive side against the wrong side of the fabric piece that is sewn together. The interfacing part should be placed against the fabric that is supposed to be on the outside of the box, but 1.5cm (⅝in) in to the lining, see figure B.

Trace the pattern to the lining piece four times, like a mirror image of the interfacing part and against the interfacing parts' edge.

Cut the whole shape, remembering to add a seam allowance to the lining.

Fold one of the boxes with lining so that it lies right sides facing against the next piece, and sew together, see figure C. Continue folding and stitch up the sides to the left. Then place the ends against each other and sew all the way around, leaving one area for reversing the lining, see figure D.

Reverse the box and close the reverse opening with tacking (basting) stitches. Push the lining into the box. Iron the box and press the folds with an iron to achieve a nice shape.

See pattern on page 45.

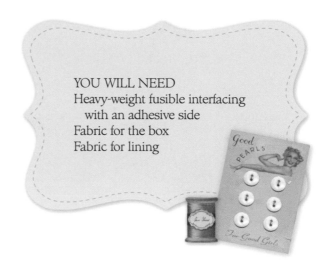

A

B

C

D

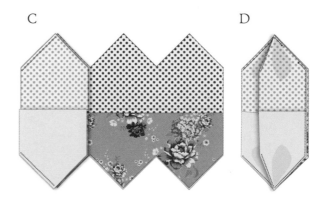

Patterns

Add seam allowance to all patterns unless instructed otherwise.

Dotted lines mark openings or splices. ES marks areas that require extra seam allowance.

Bug (pages 10-11)

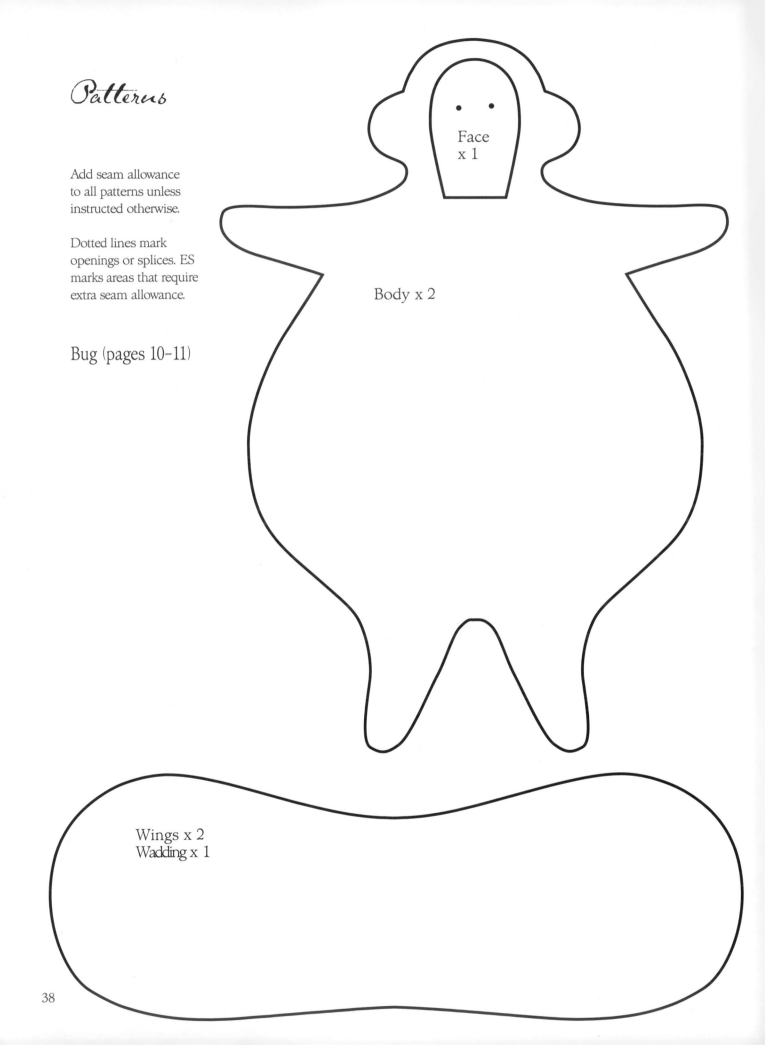

Face
x 1

Body x 2

Wings x 2
Wadding x 1

Springtime Bags
(pages 12–13)

A

B

Bag

Folding edge

A

B

Lid

Bag

Bow x 2 double

Folding edge

Bow

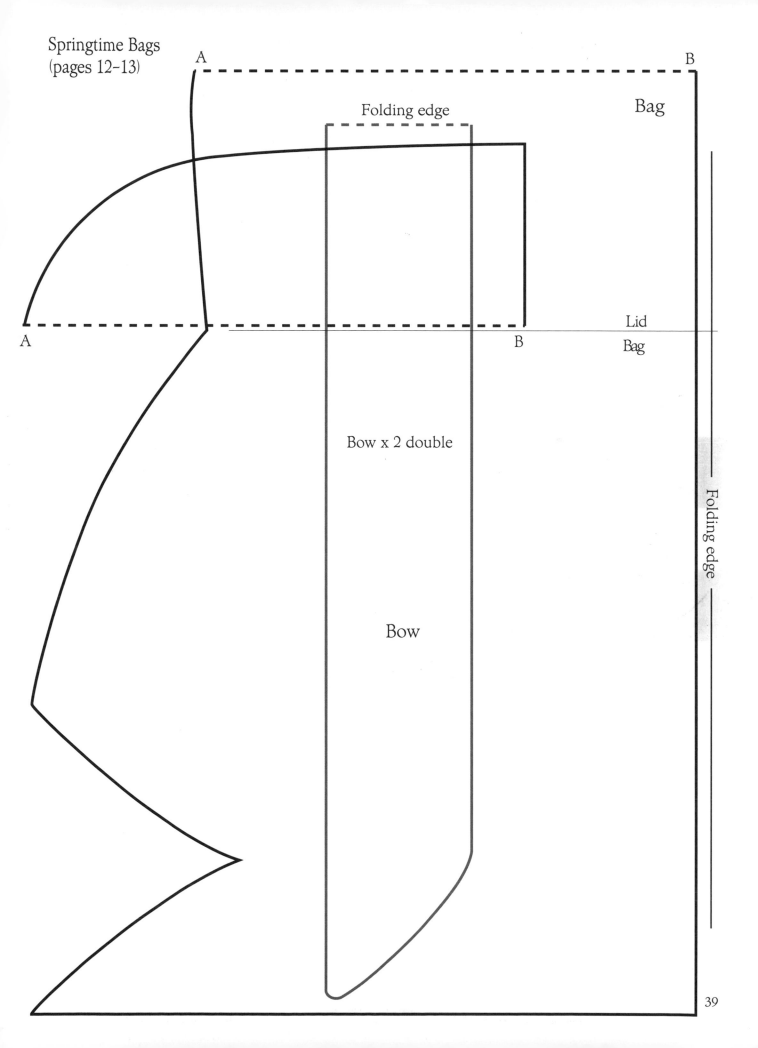

Garden Party and Sewing Angels (pages 14–19 and 31–35)
Denim Jacket (pages 17–19)

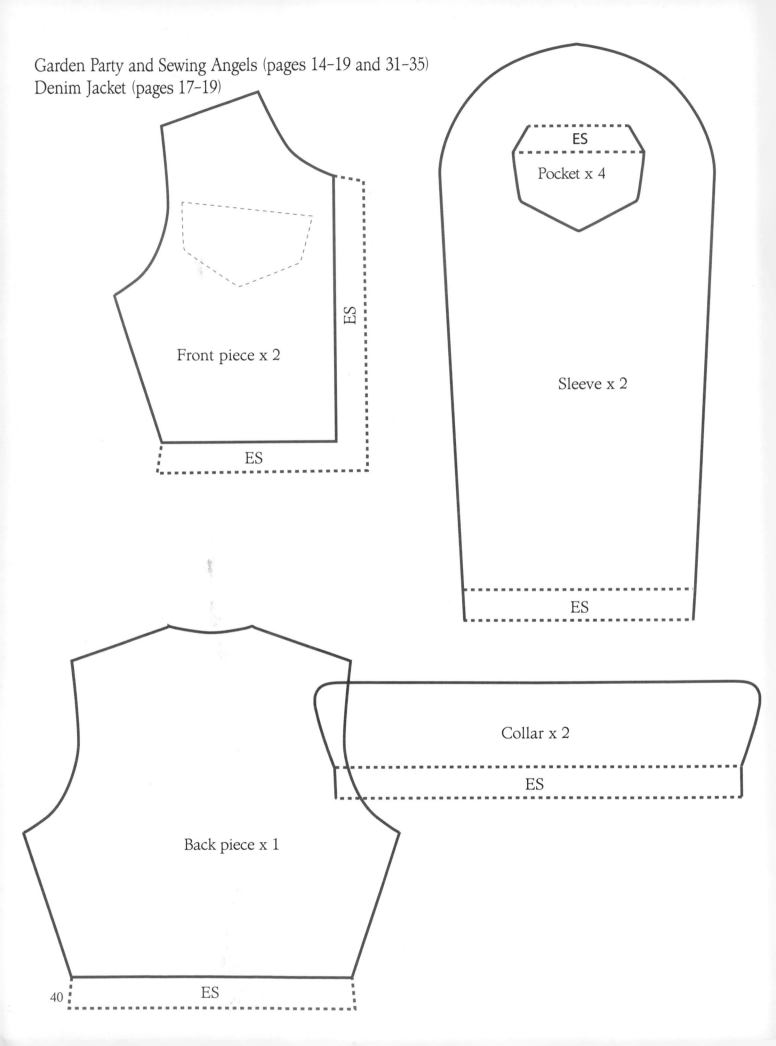

Front piece x 2

ES

ES

ES

Pocket x 4

Sleeve x 2

ES

Back piece x 1

Collar x 2

ES

ES

Garden Party and Sewing Angels (pages 14–19 and 31–35)

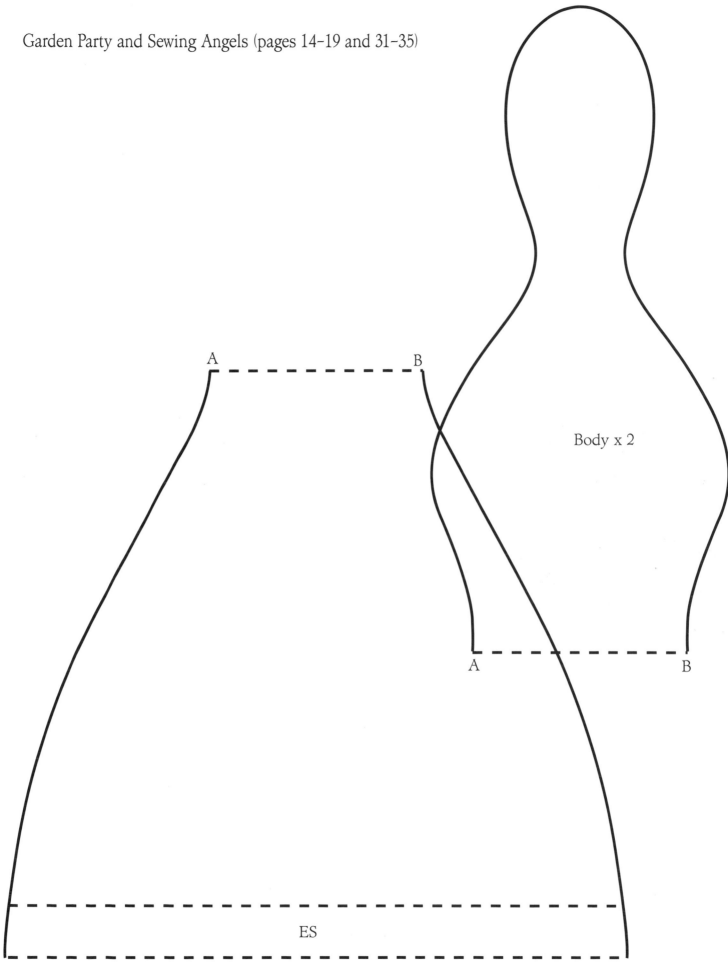

A · · · · · · B

Body x 2

A · · · · · · B

ES

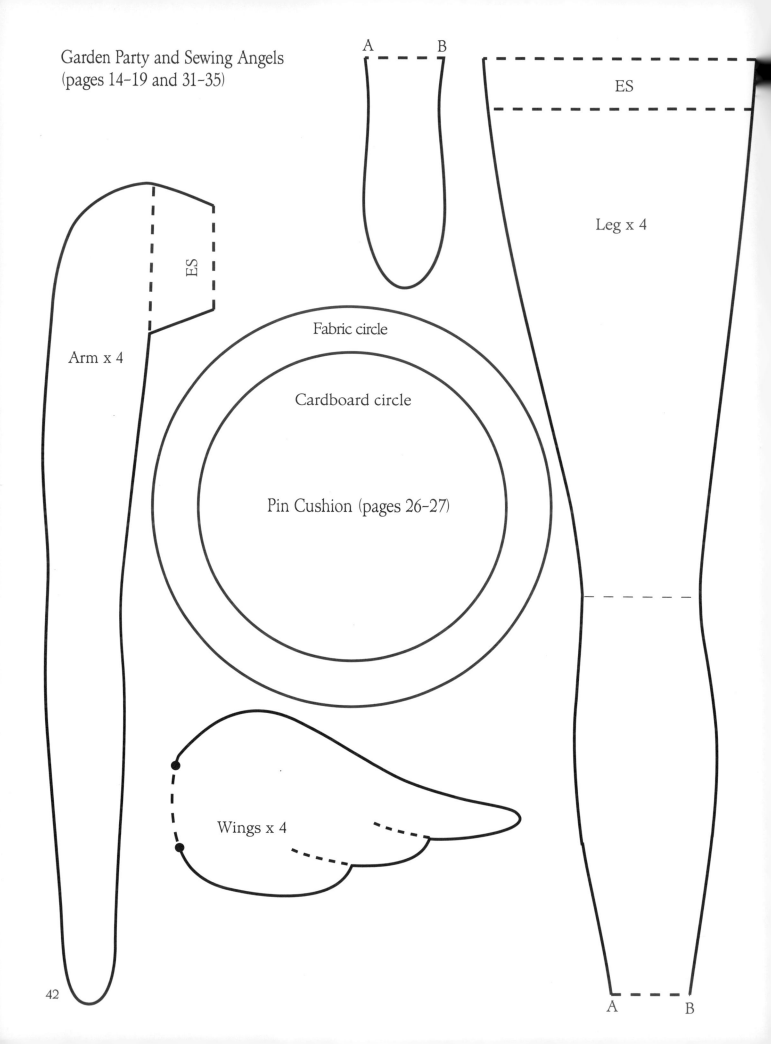

Garden Party and Sewing Angels
(pages 14–19 and 31–35)

A   B

ES

Leg x 4

ES

Arm x 4

Fabric circle

Cardboard circle

Pin Cushion (pages 26–27)

Wings x 4

A   B

42

Trousers (Pants) (pages 14–17)

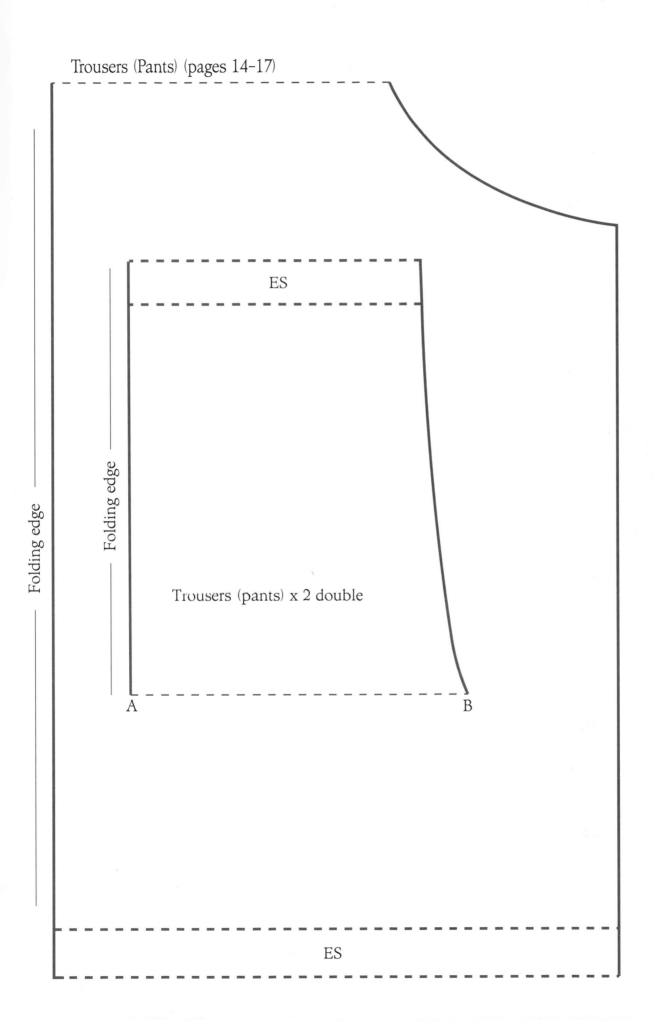

ES

Folding edge

Folding edge

Trousers (pants) x 2 double

A   B

ES

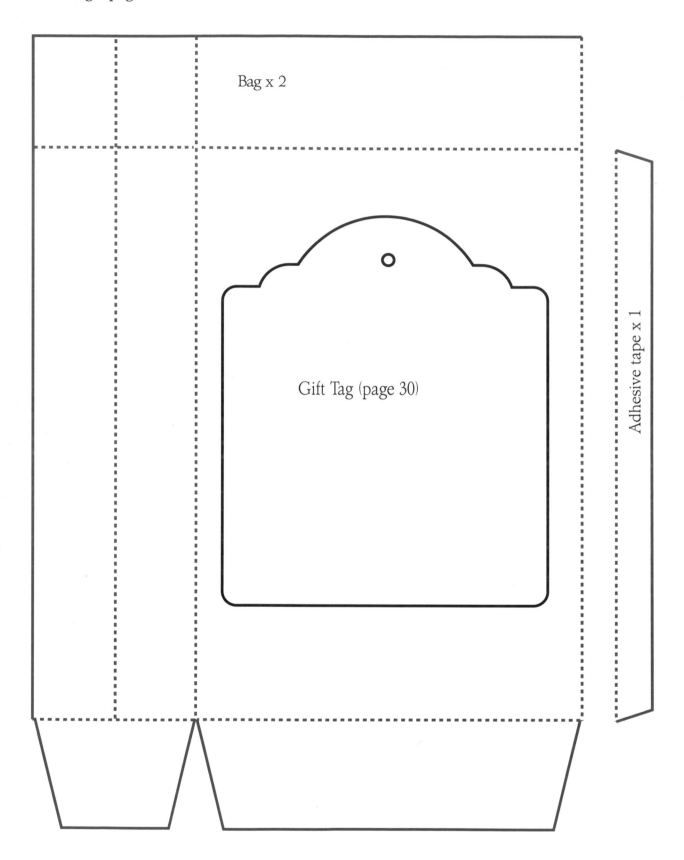

Bag x 2

Gift Tag (page 30)

Adhesive tape x 1

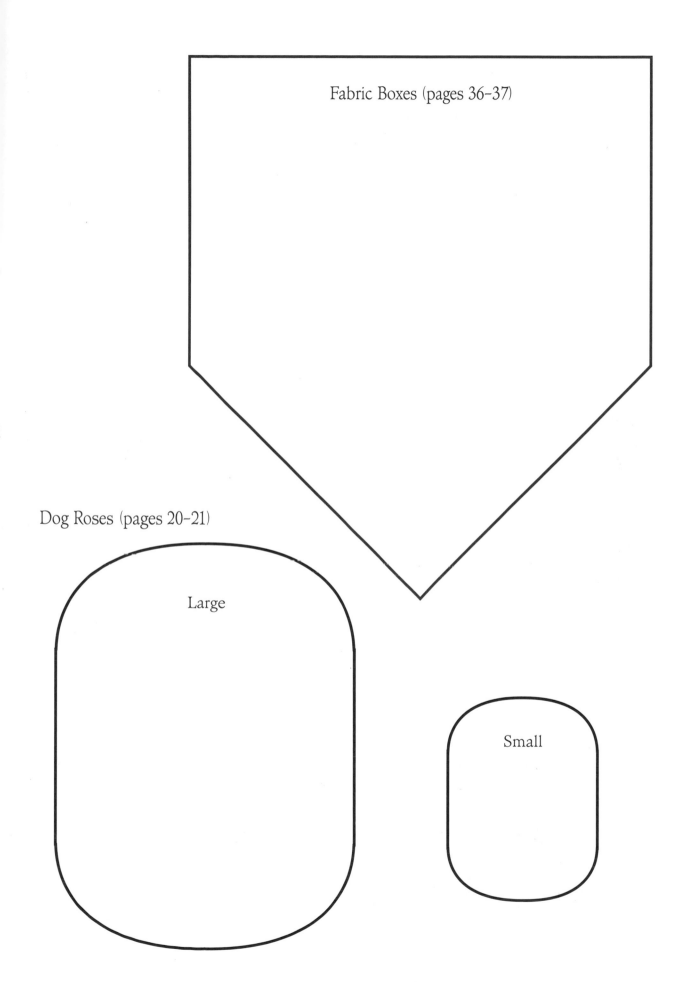

Fabric Boxes (pages 36–37)

Dog Roses (pages 20–21)

Large

Small

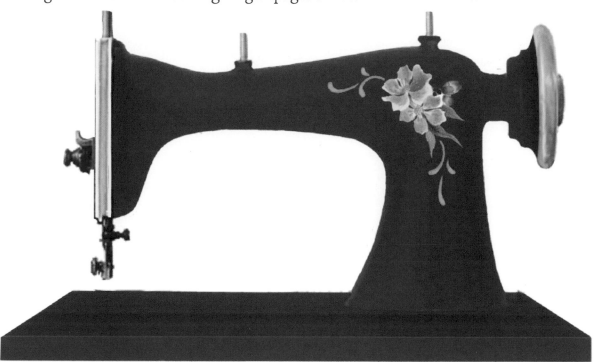

Profts

Acknowledgments

LandRomAntikk
www.landromantikk.no

Tornerose
www.tornerose.as

Mowe interiør
www.moweinterior.no

Thanks to photographer Sølvi Dos Santos and
stylist Ingrid Skaansar.
I truly appreciate your talent and patience!

Suppliers

UK

Panduro Hobby
Westway House
Transport Avenue
Brentford
Middlesex TW8 9HF
Tel: 020 8566 1680
trade@panduro.co.uk
www.pandurohobby.co.uk

Coast and Country
Crafts & Quilts
8 Sampson Gardens
Ponsanooth
Cornwall TR3 7RS
Tel: 01872 870478
www.coastandcountry
crafts.co.uk

Fred Aldous Ltd.
37 Lever Street
Manchester M1 1LW
Tel: 08707 517301
www.fredaldous.co.uk

The Fat Quarters
5 Choprell Road
Blackhall Mill
Newcastle NE17 7TN
Tel: 01207 565728
www.thefatquarters.co.uk

The Sewing Bee
52 Hillfoot Street
Dunoon
Argyll PA23 7DT
Tel: 01369 706879
www.thesewingbee.co.uk

Puddle Crafts
3 Milltown Lodge
Sandpit
Termonfeckin
County Louth
Ireland
Tel: 00353 87 355 0219
www.puddlecrafts.co.uk

Threads and Patches
48 Aylesbury Street
Fenny Stratford
Bletchley
Milton Keynes MK2 2BU
Tel: 01908 649687
www.threadsand
patches.co.uk

USA

Coats and Clark USA
PO Box 12229
Greenville
SC29612-0229
Tel: 0800 648 1479
www.coatsandclark.com

Connecting Threads
13118 NE 4th Street
Vancouver
WA 9884
www.connectingthreads.com

eQuilter.com
5455 Spine Road, Suite E
Boulder
CO 80301
www.equilter.com

Hamels Fabrics
5843 Lickman Road
Chilliwack
British Columbia
V2R 4B5
www.hamelsfabrics.com

Keepsake Quilting
Box 1618 Center Harbor
NH 03226
www.keepsakequilting.com

The Craft Connection
21055 Front Street
PO Box 1088
Onley
VA 23418
www.craftconn.com

Index